TREASURE HUNT CHALLENGES

Las Vegas Treasure Hunt Challenge

A Fast and Easy Real Life Treasure Hunt

Contents

Introduction

Welcome to the Las Vegas Treasure Hunt Challenge!
Are you ready for an adventure?
This is more than just a treasure hunt—it's a complete experience, blending excitement, creativity, and discovery. Whether you're solving puzzles, cracking codes, or following clues to uncover a secret location, **the journey itself is just as thrilling as the destination.**

· **Fast. Fun. Easy.**

Perfect for solo explorers, teams of friends, or a family outing.

· **Rediscover the thrill of exploration!**

Put down your screens, step outside, and dive into the excitement of solving unique, real-world puzzles.

· **Over $1,500 in treasures up for grabs!**

Who doesn't love the idea of uncovering hidden treasures worth hundreds of dollars?

But wait, there's more!
This challenge isn't just about the prizes. Even if the treasures have

been claimed, **the puzzles, challenges, and sense of adventure make this a rewarding experience for everyone.** Puzzle-solving enthusiasts of all kinds—whether you love crosswords, escape rooms, or real-world mysteries—will find these challenges fresh, exciting, and unforgettable.

Why Treasure Hunt Challenges?

We're passionate about secrets, surprises, and the joy of discovery. From hidden easter eggs in games and movies to solving real-life puzzles, we bring that same excitement directly to you.

- Spark your imagination.
- Embrace the thrill of discovery.
- Challenge your mind and body.

This is just the beginning—your participation today helps pave the way for **bigger adventures, tougher puzzles, and even greater prizes** in the future! **So, what are you waiting for?**

- Gather your crew or fly solo.
- Spread the word.
- Join the hunt!

How to Get Started

To embark on this thrilling adventure, your first step is to **solve the puzzles and uncover the hidden answers.** Each chapter is a unique challenge, with clues that will guide you to secret locations. Crack the codes, follow the trail, and piece it all together to locate the final object in the picture. And if the chest is still available, hurry before someone sees you!!

Are you up for the challenge? The journey awaits—let the Las Vegas Treasure Hunt Challenge begin!

For updates and treasure availability, visit @treasure_hunt_challenge702 on Instagram!

Disclaimer

Las Vegas Treasure Hunt Challenge

By participating in any part of the **Las Vegas Treasure Hunt Challenge** (hereafter referred to as "the Challenge"), you confirm that you have read, understood, and agreed to the following:

1. **Terms and Conditions**: Participation in the Challenge signifies your automatic agreement to the complete **Terms and Conditions** outlined for this contest.

2. **Do's and Don'ts**: You also agree to adhere to the rules set forth in the **Do's and Don'ts** section below.

3. **Voluntary Participation**: You acknowledge that you are voluntarily taking part in a recreational activity designed for fun. Even if all the prizes have been claimed, solving the puzzles and locating the final hidden locations remain part of the recreational enjoyment and can also serve as practice for future hunts and puzzles.

4. **Prize Announcements**: Any claimed prizes will be announced immediately after contact on the official Instagram page: **@Treasure_Hunt_C hallenge702**. Updates will also indicate which treasure chests, if any, are still available.

Do's and Don'ts Section

Dos

- Enjoy the Challenge responsibly.
- Follow all local laws and property regulations.
- Respect the natural environment and public spaces during your search.
- Solve the puzzles in the book for a fun and engaging experience.

Don'ts

- **No Digging**: Digging is not required at any location. Lightly brushing dirt away with your hand is acceptable.
- **No Trespassing on Private Property**: All treasure locations are on public property. Do not enter private property under any circumstances.
- **No Mineshafts**: Never enter a mine shaft for any reason. All locations are safe and accessible on public property.
- **No Climbing**: Treasure locations are situated in simple public walkways and hiking trails. Climbing is not required or permitted.
- **No Dangerous Activity**: The Challenge is designed to be safe. Nothing about the treasure hunt involves danger. The author and publisher are not responsible for any injuries or damages resulting from dangerous activities.
- **No Violating Curfews or Closing Times of Public Property**: If a public property has designated closing hours, you must adhere to those rules.

Las Vegas Treasure Hunt Challenge does NOT condone trespassing.

Acknowledgment of Risk

Participants agree that the Challenge is a recreational activity conducted entirely at their own risk. The author and publisher are not responsible for any injuries, damages, or losses sustained during participation.

For updates, rules, and prize announcements, follow us on Instagram: **@Treasure_Hunt_Challenge702**.

Official Rules

Terms and Conditions for the Las Vegas Treasure Hunt Skill-Based Contest

1. Introduction

Welcome to the **Las Vegas Treasure Hunt Skill-Based Contest** (hereafter referred to as "the Contest"). By participating in any part of this treasure hunt, you automatically agree to the following Terms and Conditions, including the Disclaimer and the Do's and Don'ts section. If you do not agree, you may not participate in the Contest.

Las Vegas is only the geographic location of the Contest. The City of Las Vegas is **NOT** associated with in any way or operating the Contest.

2. Eligibility

- The Contest is open to individuals aged 18 or older. Participants under 18 may participate with the supervision of a parent or legal guardian.
- The Contest is void where prohibited by law.

3. Contest Period

- The Contest begins on the release date of the book **Las Vegas Treasure Hunt** (hereafter referred to as "the Book").
- This is an open-ended contest that concludes when all three treasure chests have been found.

4. How to Participate

- Purchase a copy of **Las Vegas Treasure Hunt** on Amazon to access the puzzles and clues needed to participate.
- Participation is at your own risk, and the publisher or author are not responsible for any delays in shipping or receipt of the Book for any reason.

5. Prizes

- There are **three treasure chests**, each with $500 worth of fine .999 silver coins based on the value at the Book's release date.
- Prizes are non-transferable and cannot be exchanged for cash or other items.

6. Winner Selection

- This is a **contest of skill**, with no random or chance elements involved.
- To claim a prize:

1. Solve the puzzles and clues in your copy of **Las Vegas Treasure Hunt**.
2. Locate one of the three secret treasure chest locations.
3. Retrieve the treasure chest and contact the provided secret contact

information using the secret winning phrase.

4. Present your solved Book and the retrieved treasure chest to claim the prize.

- Winners will be announced immediately after contact on Instagram at @treasure_hunt_challenge702.
- Daily updates will be posted regarding the remaining treasures.

7. Participation Conditions

- Participation is entirely voluntary and at your own risk.
- The Contest involves no dangerous activities; all locations are on public property and situated in normal public walking or hiking areas.
- Participants agree to act responsibly and abide by all local laws and regulations.

8. Liability and Disclaimer

- The publisher and author are not responsible for:
- Injuries or damages incurred while participating in the Contest.
- Delays in shipping or receiving the Book for any reason.
- Participants assume all risks associated with participation.
- There is nothing dangerous within the Contest, and all locations are accessible to the general public.
- Las Vegas is only the geographic location of the Contest. The City of Las Vegas is **NOT** associated with in any way or operating the Contest.

9. Dispute Resolution

- All disputes arising from the Contest will be resolved through **binding arbitration** within the jurisdiction of the City of Las Vegas and Clark County, Nevada.
- This Contest is governed by the rules and regulations of a skill-based contest; therefore, no purchase necessary, Alternate Method Of Entry and sweepstakes rules and regulations **DO NOT** apply.

10. Intellectual Property and Use of Content

- By participating in the Contest, winners grant the organizer the right to use their name and likeness for promotional purposes on Instagram and other platforms without additional compensation.

11. Contact Information

- For inquiries about the Contest, contact us through Instagram at @treasure_hunt_challenge702.

12. Privacy Policy

- Any personal information collected through the Contest will be used solely for administering the Contest and will not be shared with third parties except as necessary for verification and prize distribution.

Tips

Embarking on a treasure hunt is an exciting adventure, but success comes from strategy, creativity, and persistence. Here are some tips to help you stay on track and make the most of your journey:

- **Think Outside the Box**

Treasure hunts are designed to challenge your creativity. The answers may not always be obvious, so don't be afraid to look at things from a different perspective. Be open to new ideas and unexpected solutions!

- **Don't Give Up**

Some puzzles may feel tough, but perseverance is key. Take a break if needed, clear your mind, and come back with fresh eyes. Often, the solution becomes clearer when you approach it with renewed energy.

- **The Answers Will Be Clear When You Find Them**

Once you solve a puzzle, you'll know it. Don't waste time second-guessing or wandering aimlessly for secret locations. Focus on cracking the clues first— everything else will fall into place.

- **Each Chapter Is Its Own Puzzle**

Every chapter of the hunt is self-contained with its own hidden answers leading to specific secret locations. Treat each one as a standalone challenge, and don't let previous puzzles distract you from the task at hand.

- **Stay Organized and Take Notes**

Keep track of your thoughts, solutions, and progress. Writing things down can help you see patterns or connections you might otherwise miss.

- **Work Together**

If you're hunting with a team, communicate! Different perspectives can uncover solutions faster and make the experience more enjoyable.

- **Enjoy the Journey**

Remember, the treasure is just one part of the adventure. Solving puzzles, exploring, and sharing the experience with others is just as rewarding.

- **Paperback For best experience**

For the best experience, we recommend using the paperback version. Kindle and eBook users can enhance their solving process by copying the puzzles onto paper if needed, although this step is optional.

With these tips, you'll be ready to tackle every challenge the treasure hunt throws your way. Stay sharp, stay curious, and most importantly—have fun!

Chapter 1

august 5th

The wind bites harder today. i knew the weather would turn, but it only seems fitting for the task At hand. i packed the last of the supplies at dawn, setting off alone with the chest securely strapped to my back. the Others wouldn't understand why i had to do this alone, but some things are meant to stay hidden. some things are best left unseen.

the path up was steeper than i remembered, the ground uneven and Unforgiving. it feels like each step weighs twice as much. perhaps it's the path or maybe it's the weight of what i carry—secrets wrapped in Iron and wood, waiting to be forgotten by time. i can't let anyone else find it. not Now, not ever.

at Midday, i reached the halfway ridge, where the rocks stand like ancient sentinels guarding the world. it's quiet here, save for the occasional gust of wind that whistles through the Narrow passageways, echoing in the distance like a warning. i found a place, nestled between the stones, where the earth seemed to part just enough to let me dig. the ground is firm but gives way after an hour of steady work.

the chest is buried now, deep enough that no wandering eyes will stumble upon it. i made sure to cover my tracks, though i doubt many will come this far. up here, it is forgotten. the wind carries the last echoes of my work as i begin home, leaving the treasure—and its dangers—where they belong.

```
T  E  R  U  S  A  E  R  T  D  L  O  G  V  A  U  L  T  S  E
E  D  I  G  T  S  E  H  C  S  E  T  A  N  I  D  R  O  O  C
R  T  C  L  U  E  L  S  L  E  W  E  J  P  U  Z  Z  L  E  R
C  R  S  M  E  G  S  E  A  R  C  H  D  N  I  F  P  I  T  E
E  A  R  Y  R  E  V  O  C  S  I  D  Y  E  N  R  U  O  J  V
S  P  E  P  A  T  H  T  C  A  F  I  T  R  A  E  F  A  S  O
B  E  V  P  K  O  E  X  P  E  D  I  T  I  O  N  G  A  B  C
U  D  E  A  E  S  S  A  P  M  O  C  C  I  L  E  R  P  U  N
R  I  A  M  Y  M  Y  S  T  E  R  Y  E  G  A  S  S  A  P  U
Y  H  L  E  H  C  A  C  H  U  N  T  N  O  I  T  A  C  O  L
N  E  T  T  O  G  R  O  F  H  O  A  R  D  T  P  Y  R  C  N
```

Up	Dig	Trap	Gold
Jewels	Gems	Artifact	Vaults
Hoard	Cache	Puzzle	mystery
Relic	Hide	Vault	Uncover
Reveal	Find	Key	Crypt
Search	Compass	Coordinates	Path
Journey	Discovery	Expedition	Forgotten
Passage	Hunt	Trap	Location
Safe	Pit	Bag	Treasure
Map	Chest	Clue	Secret
Bury			

Begin from the vista or don't
Either way
Take a rest about halfway
Upon the throne
Look to the right
See the rock river of white
West of the river the treasure is in sight
Now you know you are in the right place
Try to find the right rock face

_ _ _ _ ⁻_ _ _ _ _ _ _ _

Chapter 2

September Eighteen,

Today felt like a good day to set things in motion. I left around 11:00, and carefully packed everything I needed. The air had a certain crispness, not too cold but enough to wake me up fully. After breakfast, I made my way to the spot I'd been thinking about for weeks.

I found the perfect place to leave something behind, almost as if it had been waiting for me. It's tucked away, hidden from plain sight but not too far from where you might accidentally stumble upon it. I've been here a few times before, scouting, making sure the ground was just right—neither too soft nor too hard. Today, it felt different though, as if it was calling to me to finally act.

One step from the bench, I dug, not too deep, but just enough to make sure it would stay concealed for a while. A few seconds of stillness followed, and then I covered it up, carefully returning the ground to how it looked before.

As I left, I made a mental note of landmarks: a tree that looks almost like a sixteen-year-old secret and a patch of dirt that bends slightly to the west. Now, all that's left is waiting. I wonder if anyone will notice. For now, it's mine, locked away in plain sight, waiting for the right eyes to find it.

CHAPTER 2

LAS VEGAS TREASURE HUNT CHALLENGE

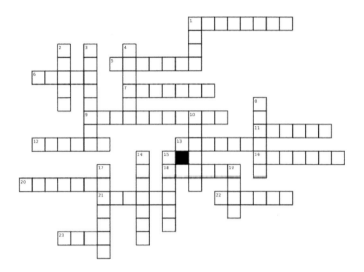

Down:

1. A small hiding place for treasure, A secret corner that conceals riches
2. A hidden supply of valuables or gold, Where treasure is secretly stored
3. Riches sought by pirates and adventurers, Gold, jewels, or valuables buried deep
4. To lock away treasure from prying eyes, Ensures treasure remains hidden and safe
8. Hidden from view, like buried gold, Describes treasure concealed in shadows
10. What you do to open a treasure chest, To reveal secrets behind a locked door
14. To secretly transport hidden riches, What pirates do with stolen loot
15. To flee with treasure in hand, What a pirate does after plundering

Across:

1. To find your way to hidden treasure, What a pirate does to steer toward riches
5. A web of hidden tunnels for escape, A system connecting secret hiding spots
6. Exchange of goods, often for treasure, Pirates may barter plunder for riches
7. To reveal hidden riches or secrets, What happens when treasure is found
9. Where treasure is often buried, Below the surface, hidden from view
11. Taken without permission, like pirate loot, Describes riches taken by stealth
12. A small chunk of gold or treasure, A prospector's prize from digging
13. Hard to find, like a secret stash, Describes treasure that evades discovery

17. A hidden spot to protect treasure, A place to shield yourself from discovery
19. A hidden danger to protect treasure, Something that ensnares would-be thieves

16. To code information about treasure's location, Pirates may use this to hide maps
18. Knowledge of hidden treasure, Something kept from others, like a map
20. The art of moving unseen to seize treasure, A skill pirates use to hide their plunder
21. A mystery or puzzle to be solved, Describes the location of hidden riches
22. A clever strategy to hide treasure, What a pirate uses to evade capture
23. A secure place for riches and secrets, Where gold and jewels are locked away

As the sunsets in the east
Find the fjord then bust
Clockwise or counter is a must
From the gaze
seven o'clock take a walk
Its not to far
From where you are
Three pillars of stone
To bring you home
Descend through time
Then ride the light beam
73 and the treasure will gleam
Shh its okay just cross the line
Its only 10ft behind

_ _ _ _ _ _-_ _ _ _

Chapter 3

Lurking shadows lanterns lit ancient alcoves, kaleidoscope light. Adventurous archaeologists eagerly engaged enigmatic labyrinths, seeking elusive artifacts. Silken sands swept softly, sealing secrets silently. Keen knowledge steps, as lost lads allure. Amidst labyrinths explorers-kindred echoed eras, eagerly engraving. Lanterns ahead, keen eyes scanned lands lost sealed away lavishly .

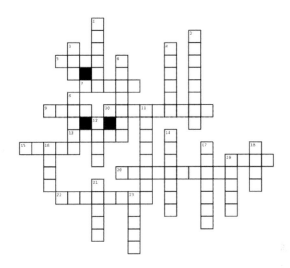

Down:

1. One who searches for hidden wealth, A treasure hunter on a daring quest
2. What adventurers carry to store treasure, Holds tools for digging and finding loot
3. A guide to hidden treasure, A pirate's most prized possession
4. Searches relentlessly for hidden fortune, Seeker of lost artifacts or riches
6. A mythical box hiding dangers and treasures, Something sealed, containing the unknown
8. A scenic view, perhaps hiding treasure, What an explorer sees from high ground
11. To unearth something hidden, like treasure, What explorers dream of doing
12. Secures the chest from prying hands, A

Across:

5. Where riches are stored securely, A treasure-filled location or side of a river
7. A large chest where riches are stored, Holds pirate loot on a ship
9. Carries treasure across the seven seas, A pirate's favorite mode of travel
10. A hidden bar of wealth in a chest, A slang term for something valuable yet idle
13. An Italian word for treasure, hidden away, A secret hoard awaiting discovery
15. A river's end, hiding secrets in the silt, A triangular landform where treasure might be lost
19. A hidden danger guarding treasure, A snare to protect or catch thieves
20. A seeker of gold and hidden secrets,

mechanism guarding secrets or riches

14. What pirates take when they find gold, Treasure claimed in a daring raid

16. What lights the way to buried treasure, A beacon for explorers in the dark

17. Luck, or the goddess who smiles upon treasure hunters, What you need to strike it rich

18. A long tale of treasure and adventure, Stories pirates share of their exploits

19. A trail leading to treasure or secrets, What explorers follow in their quest

21. Keeps a treasure map tightly rolled, Holds valuables together securely

23. To prepare for a treasure hunt, Provide tools for the daring explorer

Someone on a journey to find riches

22. One who ventures to find lost treasure, A discoverer of new lands and riches

The namesake says
Go 300 degrees
Take a seat please
But you cant laydown
Get up and walk around
1 2 3 or 4
Search inside
The treasure yours

2 x _ _ _ _ _ - _ _ _ _

Follow @Treasure_Hunt_Challenge702
Instagram

TREASURE_HUNT_CHALLENGE702

Made in the USA
Las Vegas, NV
21 December 2024

15119715R00020